CW00449458

KING'S CORONATION

Colour this in :-)

TIME CAPSULE BOOK

BY FRANCES ROSE

♡ Dedicated to my personal penguin: Nicholas ♡

Please share and tag me in your creations on Instagram @frances_rose55

Copyright Frances Rose 2023

www.frances-rose.com

WHAT IS A TIME CAPSULE BOOK?

The Coronation of their Majesties King Charles III and Queen Camilla is set to take place on 6th May 2023, and this Time Capsule Book provides a way to record this special moment in time.

Did you know that Queen Victoria kept a diary? She started it when she was 13 and she wrote her final entry 69 years later, just before she died, aged 81. The 43,765 pages provide a fantastic insight into life in the Victorian times as well as the key events in her life, including her Coronation. Queen Victoria's diary is extra special because she also included illustrations and stuck interesting items onto the pages.

It is Queen Victoria's fabulous diary that gave me the idea for this Time Capsule Book! A place to document the King and Queen's Coronation, as well as life in 2023. On each page you are given a prompt, and your challenge is to respond to it by writing, drawing, doodling, colouring, collaging, sticking, taking photos – whatever you like, so long as you are having fun and being creative! Once it's complete, you will have a book that brings together the present moment for future generations to read and discover – your own little piece of Coronation history.

TIPS FOR USING THIS BOOK...

The pages of this book are a tad thin, but never fear – I am here to save the day and give you some tips and tricks on how to make it work:

The best materials to use are the kind that are less likely to show through a page e.g. crayons, colouring pencils and crafty bits (like glitter, googly eyes, stickers, etc).

If you do fancy using wet media (like paint and felt tips), then the best thing to do is to create your artwork on a separate piece of paper and stick it in afterwards.

Underneath the prompts, I have included ideas. You can choose to use them or completely ignore them and do it your own way.

LET'S GET STARTED...

This book belongs to: Age:

Date started: Date completed:

Progress tracker (colour in a circle every time you complete a prompt):

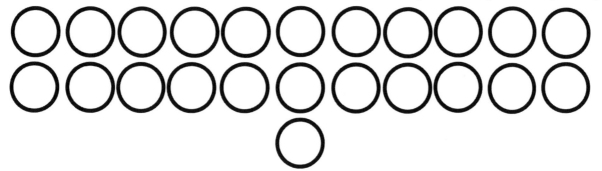

CREATE

A

SELF-PORTRAIT

What do you look like in 2023?

A BIT ABOUT YOU

You might want to include: the things that you really enjoy doing; your favourite colour, food, TV shows, films, music, places to visit and people.

WHERE DO YOU LIVE?

Create a page about where you live!

Ideas: a picture of your abode, a floor plan, a map, photographs of your village/town or a drawing of a famous local landmark.

YOUR
FAMILY
AND FRIENDS

Create a page about your family and friends!

Idea: draw cartoons of them or create a photo collage.

A

TYPICAL

DAY IN

YOUR LIFE

Create a diary entry/cartoon strip to depict a typical day in your life!

2023

FACTS

Tell us more about what things are like in 2023! Who is the prime-minister? Who are the other world leaders? What have been the top news stories so far this year? Who is in the music charts? What's happening in your favourite sport? How much do things like milk, bread, stamps, petrol, cinema tickets cost?

CREATE A CORONATION INVITATION

The King and Queen's official invitations included illustrations of flowers and nature – the King's interests – can you incorporate this into your design too? You could even photocopy your invitations and use them to invite people to your own coronation celebrations.

DESIGN A CROWN

Add sparkle!

CREATE A PORTRAIT OF KING CHARLES III

CREATE A
PORTRAIT OF
QUEEN
CAMILLA

CREATE A FACT FILE ABOUT KING CHARLES

Research King Charles III and then present the information as creatively as possible.

CREATE A FACT FILE ABOUT QUEEN CAMILLA

Research Queen Camilla and then present the information as creatively as possible.

THE ROYAL

FAMILY TREE

Research and draw the Royal Family tree.

A KING

OR

QUEEN

FROM HISTORY

Pick your favourite king or queen from history. Then, get creative in whatever way you fancy! Ideas: write a song or poem about them; draw, paint, collage their portrait or depict a key moment in their life.

SCRAPBOOK NEWSPAPER ARTICLES ABOUT THE CORONATION

JOURNAL OF
6TH MAY 2023

Keep a diary or create a cartoon strip of 6th May 2023 – Coronation Day.

COLLAGE OF PHOTOGRAPHS FROM YOUR CORONATION CELEBRATIONS

CORONATION
MEMORABILIA

A place to stick any tickets, leaflets and any other Coronation memorabilia.

NEW
MONEY

New coins will feature the King's head. Can you find every denomination of the new coins/notes and create wax rubbings or drawings of them here?

NEW

POSTBOXES

New postboxes will have CR (Charles Rex) embossed onto it.

Idea: stick a photograph of the first one that you see here!

START A STAMP COLLECTION

Stamps will feature the new King's head.

Every time you receive one with a king on, stick it here!

TEN YEAR

PREDICTIONS

Write a list of things that you think will happen over the next ten years,
either in your personal life or in the world generally.
Ten years from now, you can look back on the list to see if you were right!

WRITE A LETTER TO CONGRATULATE THE KING & QUEEN

Use the following pages to write a letter (cut the pages out of the book or use the space for a first draft).

The address to write to the King and Queen can easily be found online.

If you receive a response, which people often do, stick it into this book.

Printed in Great Britain
by Amazon

21677331R00029